Take Time
To Smell the Roses
Book of Poetry

By

Robert Richey

Enjoy this Book

Bob Rich

ISBN: 1-4033-4471-X (e-book)
ISBN: 1-4033-4472-8 (Paperback)
ISBN: 1-4033-8753-2 (Hardcover)

This book is printed on acid free paper.

1stBooks – rev. 11/7/02

Introduction

When the author of this collection of poems was a young man he ventured out on the open sea for six years. During that time he saw all the various moods that the waters can display.

There are times when the ocean can be a place of utter peace and calm, with little if any chop. The winds can be like gentle zephyrs and with air that is crisp and clear. The sky above can be the most beautiful azure imaginable while the sea which reflects the sky can be the richest of indigo hue. On such a day there is no more beautiful place on earth.

But the open sea can be like a capricious mistress whose mood swings are never predictable. And yet the latent power and mindless ferocity that lies just beneath the surface attracts some men like a magnet and they return again and again to thrill to its allure and charm. For it is only on the Open Sea, that the viewer in such a sacred moment witnessing such a celestial awe inspiring panorama, will feel closer to God than anywhere else on earth.

Then again without warning the winds can begin to increase in violence. The water being lashed by the wind become more and more disturbed and the waves build up into watery mountains towering a hundred feet high.

Even the biggest most powerful vessel conceived of and built by the hand of man is helpess when caught up in such a cauldron of violence. Heading into the wind and the waves is a matter of life and death. To veer either to port or starboard or try to run with the winds is to invite disaster.

To broach is to wallow briefly in the trough before capsizing and sinking into a watery grave.

Even a ship as big as a battleship can be like a bit of flotsam caught up in the flood. It will toboggan down the trailing slope of the preceding wave only to knife it's bow into the face of the advancing wave. Burying itself so deeply it virtually comes to a halt. Then after a brief pause the bow drunkenly starts to rise as the propellers try vainly to drive it forward. The turbines whine and groan with stresses far above the designers red-line. Just before it breaks the surface, near the crest of the wave, green water thunders and crashes down the foc'sle smashing all in its path. Then the bow protruding out unsupportedly into the salty air, comes crashing down sending tons of water skyward. Tilting precariously downward the propellers rise up out of the water and spin wildly. Then as the vessel plunges downward again the propellers regain their purchase and the sudden shock causes massive surges of pulsations to wrack the hull. After many hours perhaps even days of this sort of punishment the weary seafarer thinks longingly of the Man from Galilee who calmed the angry waves on the Sea of Galilee saying only, "Peace be still." And to his companions saying, "Oh ye of little faith." And his disciples marveled among themselves saying, "What manner of man is this that even the winds and the waves obey him?"

Below the equator the ocean is warm and humid. It has an unworldly aura not to be found anywhere else. At night at sea with no moon or clouds is to sail thru inky darkness. Masses of phosphorous glow in the water and with a full moon out flying fish can be seen gliding from crest to crest of the waves in the ghostly light. Occasionally a lunar rainbow will appear when the atmospheric conditions are right. Sailing under darken ship conditions with no man made lights to detract from the scene is breath taking. The stars in the firmament are so bright and so numerous that it literally surfeits the viewers mind. Their glory and magnificence leaves memories that linger in the mind of the viewer for a lifetime.

In the inky darkness where danger can lurk just over the rim of the sea there is a certain degree of comfort knowing the all seeing eye of Radar will detect any foe who may wish them ill harm and provide a brief moment to decide to flee or fight.

As one stands there in awe and wonder at the gloriousness of the scene it seems a small door in a recess of the mind opens just a whisper and a tiny childs voice begins reciting lines from childhood, "Twinkle twinkle little star; how I wonder what you are; way above the world so high like a diamond in the sky." And then from childhood the mind recalls words recited while kneeling by ones bedside with the parent, "Now I lay me down to sleep. I pray the Lord my soul to keep. If I should die before I wake, I pray the Lord my soul to take. Amen." For in times of extreme stress a man must draw strength from within himself if he is survive or retain his sanity.

In times of extreme peril when young men venture into harms way one finds there are no atheist. Either one finds comfort in faith and hope otherwise lies madness. And from the past again that still small voice seems to recite, "Let not your heart be troubled. Ye believe in God believe also in me. In my fathers house are many mansions. If it were not so I would have told you. I go to prepare a place for you and if I go I will return again and take you unto myself. For

I am the truth and the life. He who believeth in me shall never die." Comfort was also found in one of the Psalms, "Ye though I walk thru the Valley of Death I will fear no evil for tho' art with me. Thy rod and thy staff they comfort me."

Any reader of this collection of poetry will find threads of that time at sea woven throughout the fabric of this work. And that should not be too surprising.

It is the writer's hope that these poetic lines will provide inspiration, comfort and encouragement to a reader who at the moment may be discouraged or bowed down in grief or where a cherished goal has always been just out of reach. For it has been said. "It is always darkest just before the dawn."

Take Time...

Take time to smell the roses
Take time along the way
Take time to pause and wonder
Take time to work, but take time to play

Take time to view the heavens
Take time at night on the open sea
Take time on a desert night
Take time to marvel at eternity

Take time to know what you are viewing
Take thought while standing on this earth
Take in all that you are seeing
Take in the universe, light years before your birth

Take time to help a neighbor
Take time to listen to a mourning dove
Take time to say a blessing
Take time to fall in love

Take time to acknowledge your creator
Take time though you may often be in pain
Take time above all else to smell the roses
Take time so that you will not have lived in vain

Robert Richey

A Candle in the Wind

There are those who believe
In the theory of evolution
And that as concerns creation
There is no other solution

They also believe that
Man descended from the ape
And that any other theory
Is hopelessly out of date

But if we listen only to the mocking bird
And are not thrilled by the lark
Then if a beam of light didn't last forever
Wouldn't the universe be dark?

And if we are children of God
And truly believe, and not just pretend
Then won't we be like the beam of light
Not just a candle in the wind?

A Celestial Spring

A leaf dry and sere
Newly dropped from oft the tree
Severed from the leafy bough
Having fulfilled it's destiny

Crafted of twigs, a feather here and there
A robin's nest high up; held fast
The young birds having winged away
Awaiting winters cold and icy blast

A tree framed against the sky
Nestled on the earth below
Patiently bidding it's time
Awaiting winter's fluffy snow

Not like the leaf or the nest of twigs
But like the tree; what life will bring
We too shall don glorious raiment
When arrives that Celestial Spring

A Devoted Friend

One of the greatest gifts
That God can send
To each of us
Is a loyal friend

A friend who always
Greets us with a radiant smile
And is willing to travel with us
That extra mile

A friend who is always there
One who is true beyond belief
When all else fails
To comfort us in grief

A friend whose face
Lights up the place
And ever greets us
With a warm embrace

Yes, one of the greatest gifts
That God can send
To warm our hearts
Is a loyal and loving friend

A Dream

When I was just a boy
I fell in love one day
And that love has only deepened
In every passing way

I fell in love with a dream
That within itself has a sequel
A dream dedicated to the proposition
That all men are created equal

A dream that has sustained us
Through all the passing years
And continues to sustain us
In times of grief and tears

A dream that lifts our hearts
Up higher than the skies
A dream that helps us view
The future through hopeful eyes

A dream that will fight evil
Every place it can
And I thank God
For the privilege of being
born an American

Robert Richey

A Highway in the Sky

It was a raw chill winter night
The earth dozed peacefully 'neath the snow
While the icicles that graced the boughs
Gently swayed to and fro

The wind's icy breath knifed thru the canopy
Now gusting fast now gusting slow
While the pheasants burrowed deeper
Seeking warmth beneath the snow

From a far off distant knoll
There came a lonesome coyote's howl
And through the darkling glade
Swiftly and silently glided a hooting Owl

The stars in the firmanent on high
Shone down as they had since time began
In their glory and magnificence
As they had long before the advent of man

There was a shout from up above
It rang out loud and clear
And there on the Highway in the Sky
Was Santa and his reindeer

A True Friend

If you would like to find a friend
One who would always be loyal and true
A friend who could be depended on
To always be faithful to you

If you would like to find a friend
One who would be there night or day
When you most needed them
While all others walked away

If you would like to find a friend
Devoted to you as long as they might live
That very special kind of friend
With an infinite capacity to forgive

If you would like to find a friend
Who will never be argumental
Who will never find fault with you
Or who will never be judgemental

If you would like to find a friend
One who is dependable day or night
Who already feels lonely for you
Even before you are out of sight

If these qualities you admire the most
The kind of friend you would pray God to send
Then to be deserving of such devotion
It requires that you too must be such a friend

Robert Richey

<u>Along the Way</u>

Life is like a journey
That can carry us near or far
But can we reach our destination
If we followeth not a constant star?

For the foxes have their holes
And the birds of the air their nests
However they are imprinted
In all their individual quests

But a child must early learn
The difference between right and wrong
If he is to develop a conscience
That elevates him above the throng

For there are those who only
Consider when its time to pick and choose
What they stand to gain
Versus what they stand to lose

A man may be wildly successful
Receiving accolades day after day
Yet find the most rewarding thing of all
Was the friendships he made along the way

A Thing of Beauty
Is a joy forever
words by John Keats

<u>A Tie That Binds</u>

The magic of the spoken word
A gift from up above
Is a gossamer strand that binds us
In friendship and in love

<u>The Sunrise</u>

As the day is slowly dying
And the shadows start to fall
With the sun diving into the abyss
The night birds begin to call

The moon sails on majestically
Across the sky so vast
While the stars beam down beatifically
As they have for eons past

T'is then the night hawk
And the owl glide silently on their way
With malevolence in their glances
As they search for their nightly prey

The night creatures furtively
Venture on their hurried way
To complete their nocturnal rounds
Before the break of day

Then appears the glory of the sunrise
With divine colors of mother-of- pearl
Like unto tinted sails on the ocean
As they slowly and gently ufurl

Our lives are like the sunrise
And like the sunset on the sea
We appear out of the darkness
And venture into eternity

Robert Richey

The sun is ever blameless
Whereas we have been born in sin
Yet like the sun, which dies each evening
At sunrise, we too shall be born again

Before the Throne

A bounteous bouquet of roses
Ephemeral beauty does not last
It's fragrant perfume permeates the air
Then it too fades into the past

The summer shower that quenches
The thirst of the parched land
Is like unto you and I when
A stranger offers us a helping hand

A cheerful smile and a warm embrace
We have many times been told
Is not only imperative for the young
But also for the very old

If in scaling the ladder of success
We are rewarded a thousand fold
Yet find that casting bread upon the waters
May be more valuable than gold

If we expend our entire lives
In achieving fame and success
In the end will it be worth it
If we fail to find happiness

Perhaps in the end it matters not
All the money and wealth we may accrue
Because we may very well find
You cannot take it with you

13

Robert Richey

On the Judgement Day
When we stand before the Throne
Will we be surrounded by our friends
Or will be standing there, All Alone

<u>Broken Dreams</u>

The landscape was bathed in moonlight
While a canopy of stars glittered above
It happened one night in spring
A perfect time to fall in love

They were swept up in a youthful passion
While time itself seemed to stop
And for a few exciting wonderful moments
He stood high on the mountain top

But with the first harsh rays of the sun
Heralding the onset of a new day
The dreams turned into ashes
And a cold wind swept them away

Robert Richey

By Grace Alone

When I see a man shuffling down the street
With his clothes all grimy and worn
I can't help thinking that to him
Life must be like a thorn

When I see a man shuffling down the street
All downcast and utterly forlorn
Who is wondering what his life is all about
Wondering why he was ever born

When I see a man shuffling down the street
Where all hope has flown away
Who probably never ever looks back
To the time of a happier day

When I see a man shuffling down the street
As weary and lonely and outcast as he can be
I can't help thinking, but for the Grace of God
That outcast man could be Me!

Cast Thy Bread

It has been said in days of old
A Tale that has 'oft been told
Cast thy bread upon the waters
It shall be returned a thousand fold

Always striving to do our best
In scaling the lofty heights
Of our own Mount Everest
Ne'er prone to fancy flights

Ne'er divining we had a prayer
Yet striving without a stop
To what new goals do we aspire
When we stand on the mountain top?

If we successfully vault the rung
Receiving plaudits from near and far
Shall we merely bask in adulation
Or just quietly turn and raise the bar?

Tho' Our pathway through life
Be it wide or narrow
Knowing God keeps his eye
Even on the sparrow

May hope with us always abide
With faith keeping us company
Assured that there is a celestial plan
For each of us in eternity

Robert Richey

<u>Disenchantment</u>

The hopes and dreams of yesteryear
Have faded with the past
The pledges and promises that we made
To each other did not last

It never dawned upon us when
We vowed ever to be true
That the day would come we would find
We'd entertain a different view

For swept up in youthful passion
Where it seemed 'twas all to gain
Not realizing that in the end
'Twould only bring us pain

And yet although I find
I have feelings of regret
Yet find I look back fondly
To the wondrous night we met

Heavens Gates

It's a Time of mistletoe and holly
And presents 'neath the tree
Of carols sung in the frosty air
And about the nativity

It's about warm embraces by
Those most important in our life
Who have always been there
In times of trouble and of strife

It's about chestnuts being roasted
And toasted over a roaring fire
While we cuddle in a blanket
With the one we most desire

It's the christmas table spread with
A bountiful sumptuous repast
Accompanied by a grateful prayer
For all the blessings of the past

For it's the celebration of the birthday
Of the one we hold most sanctified
Whose death and resurrection
Opened the gates of heavens, wide

Hidden Away

When I was just a boy
I learned about elves and fairies
And learned early on
That lifes not always a bowl of cherries

When I was just a boy
I learned about Tipperary
And about the easter bunny
And about the tooth fairy

When I was just a boy
I was told it was better to work than to beg
And learned how to fly a kite
And how to play mumbly peg

When I was just a boy
I was taught to honor my father and mother
And that we should all strive
To love one another

When I was just a boy
I learned to play a game called tag
To pledge allegiance too
And salute the Flag

But when I was a young man
And walked the earth and sailed the sea
When I walked thru the valley of death
I believe that God watched over me

Now that I am old
And my hair has turned gray
I find many of my dreams of the past
Have silently slipped away

Yet now tho' I am old
Hope and faith with me still abides
And once in awhile I catch a glimpse
Of that little boy hidden away inside

My Land...

It's the bonniest of lands we have My Lad
The bonniest that there can ever be
It stretches from north to south a tad
And east to west from sea to shining sea

And we have the bonniest of crews My Lad
To man our magnificent ship of state
They've been tried in good times and in bad
My lad and never found wanting Mate

And the secret My Lad of this great land
Is as plain as it can ever be
It's in the willingness to lend a hand
And their boundless love of liberty

But liberty and freedom go hand in hand
One can not be had without the other
Each lover of truth must always stand
Beside all other men as a brother

There is one cardinal fact of life
In time we all eventually see
That amid all the turmoil and strife
Of life freedom never does come free

Someone has always had to pay the price
Of the suffering and bleeding and pain
Someone else must toss the losing dice
So all the rest of us can gain

The debt we owe this bold brave band
Without question we can never repay
The least that we can do is lend a hand
And honor all of them on Veterans Day

Robert Richey

I Know Not...

I know not what the 'morrow will bring
But the flowers will bloom
And the birds will sing

I know not how high the corn will grow
But with winter's icy breath
There will be snow

I know not when the groundhog will appear
But there will be surf at the beach
And foam on the beer

I know not where trade winds may play
But know that they will
Drive sails along their way

I know not what the fates will spawn
But there is one irrefutable fact
Time Marches On!

<u>Life is…</u>

Life is like a river flowing to the sea
Life is like a river flowing thru eternity

There's just no way to stem it
No way to stop the raging tide
No way to swim against it
So just sit back and enjoy the ride

The moon beams down upon us
The sun shines from up above
But the most important things in life
Are hope and faith and love

For all of those who live their lives
And try to do their best
It's comforting to know that
We all ride the rivers crest

For Life is like a river flowing to the sea
Life is like a river flowing thru eternity

<u>Lifes Pathway</u>

If the pathway leads o'er the mountain
Fraught with peril tho' it may seem
Can the wanderer ever reach the summit
If he followeth not a dream?

If life is at the flood stage
And there is no safe place to hide
Should one swim 'gainst the current
Or drift idly with the tide?

For a life without a purpose
Is like a yacht without a sail
Or like an Knight Errant
Without a Holy Grail

Is it sufficient just to
Breathe in and breathe out
And live a life of hope
Or one filled with fear and doubt?

Would his response still be today
As to the young rich man's plaintive plea
Go, give all that thy hath to the poor
And take up thy cross and follow me

For it was once said
A long long time ago
Where a man's treasure is
So will his heart be also

When that fateful hour arrives
On bended knee will we hear the words
Oh, Good and faithful servant
I am well pleased with thee

<u>Life's Stormiest Seas</u>

In everyone's voyage thru life
There may be times of utter tranquility
At other times be fraught with peril
As they sail thru life's stormiest seas

There may be times of deepest despair
As they watch a loved one's life slip away
Finding comfort only in believing that
Their paths will cross again one day

There are those who live their lives
Seemingly carefree and debonair
Yet they too may find one day
They have their own cross to bear

No man is an island unto himself
It has been said; and we too may divine
Coming to realize one day
That we are immersed in all mankind

But if we persevere and stay the course
And embrace our beliefs with ardor
Then the Great Captain of us all
One day, will bring us to safe harbor

<u>Moments</u>

The splendor of the rainbow
The faraway cooing of the dove
The magic of the moonlight
The awe inspiring firmament above

The grandeur of the mountains
The quiet murmur of the brook
The peaceful stroll in a garden
The tryst in a cozy nook

The glory of the sunset
The soft patter of the rain
The haunting hooting of the owl
The mocker's melodic refrain

All these precious moments
Never go out of style
Yet each in it's own way
Makes living more worthwhile

Robert Richey

<u>My Country is to Me</u>

My country is to me
The one place on earth
Above all else
I shall always desire to be

My country is to me
Like a maiden, demure and chaste
Always with an aura about her
Of beauty and of grace

My country is to me
Like a good shepherd
Watching o'er the fold
Providing a haven
For the weak, the sick
and the very old

My country is to me
Like a guardian angel
Looming 'gainst the sky
With her torch of freedom
Always held on high

My country is to me
A verdant land stretching
From sea to shining sea
Always searching and striving
For justice and equality

My country is to me
The land of the brave,
The beautiful, the bold
Where breathing the heady
Air of freedom is deemed
More valuable than gold

My country is to is me
The provider to those of
High or low degree
The boundless blessings and
The irresistible lure of
Opportunity

My country is to me
The domain of the eagle
and the dove
And I shall always look up
To Her in adoration
With awe, and wonder
And an abiding love

"Viva America!"

Robert Richey

<u>True Love</u>

Take a beam of moonlight
Add a drop of dew
Blend with the fragrance of blossoms
And prepare a heavenly brew

Take a pair of lovers
In a special world all their own
Clinging closely to each other
Saying, "Goodnight" until dawn

Seeing in each others eyes
Happiness that will never fade
One of lifes natural wonders
The way of a man with a maid

<u>**Relativity**</u>

A man may walk in sunshine
And again he may walk in rain
He may experience ecstasy
Or perhaps experience pain

He may climb a mountain
Or break the tape in a race
He may take home the trophy
Or maybe just fall on his face

He may have lofty dreams
And by ambition be consumed
He may be completely despondent
Or at times feel he is doomed

But regardless of what happened
If he never could forgive
Or if he never fell in love
Did he ever really live?

Robert Richey

<u>Rhapsody of Love</u>

Your Eyes are like the stars above
Your lips like cherry wine
E'en Jove sipping of a nectar cup
Can ne'er compare with thine

The magical aura of your being
The winsomeness of your smile
Your tender touch and warm embrace
Make life for me worthwhile

I am grateful that I found you
That fate brought you my way
But now that we are together
Happiness is here to stay

There is an infinite joy in knowing
That you alone were meant for me
Hearing you whisper "I love you"
Fulfills my greatest fantasy

<u>Take Heart</u>

If haunted by the specter of extinction
And the pathway we must tread

Take heart in knowing

That with the butterfly newly on the wing
Only the chrysalis is dead

Robert Richey

<u>The Greatest Gift of All</u>

Christmas is the Birthday
Of the Man from Galilee
He expunged all the Faithful's Sins
When he died upon the Tree

Oh Death where is thy Sting
Oh Grave where is thy Victory
For in His Resurrection
He forever set All Believers Free

And in that glorious Hereafter
There will be no pain or regret
For in that blissful Second Eden
The Sun will never set

And we shall all be together
In a Life that never ends
Secure and Happy in the Bosom
Of our Family and our Friends

So join in the Celebration
Of the Gift so dearly Won
For God so loved the World
That He gave his only Begotten Son

<u>Temptation</u>

There is a temptation to judge others
By the garments that they wear
The way they walk and talk
Or the way they fix their hair

There is a temptation to judge others
About the company they keep
The way they squander money
Or snore when they are asleep

There is a temptation to judge others
Who balk when the chips are down
Never taking life seriously
Always acting like a clown

There is a temptation to judge others
Questioning the life style that they choose
But the person doing the criticizing
Never walked in the other person's shoes

Thats Life

If it seems life's is too much for you
And has really, really got You down
Where You've forgotten how to smile
And only seem to know how to frown

Then pause and look all around
And take a moment or two
For You will surely find that
There are Others worse off than You

Perhaps there is a reason
So we shouldn't put up a fuss
And maybe this is God's way
Of individually testing Us

For it is easy being a winner
And not much fun getting beat
Maybe it's not how we handle victory
But rather how we accept defeat

One lesson to be learned
Whether We are happy or sad
Is how to go about taking the good
Right along with the bad

For life never made Us a promise
That it would always be peaches and cream
Or that We would always ride around
In a gilded coach or a fancy limousine

For even in the Garden of Eden
Adam found that Satan had horns
And if We want to enjoy the roses
We must learn to put up with the thorns

Will it matter the most at the pearly gate
Whether we achieved success and fame
Or garnered medals made of gold
But rather will it be; How We played the game?

Robert Richey

The Dawn of a New Day

The earth in it's ponderous journey
Is a captive in the sun's warm embrace
Twirling like a whirling dervish
On it's curvalinear path through space

The spinning earth gives birth to
The sunrise and the sunset as well
As it rotates upon it's axis
Each one casting yet another spell

With the moon long past the zenith
And the Shades of Night beginning to fade
Of ebony, mauve and gray that permeates
The surrounding forest and the glade

The plaintive cooing of the dove
Emanating from both dale and hill
Supplants the haunting lilting notes
Of the foraging whippoorwill

The first tender tendrils of light
That probe the eastern sky
Are harbingers of the early morn'
Heralding that dawn is nigh

Then as the old day is dying
Having fulfilled it's destiny
The sun appears in the eastern sky
In all it's glorious majesty

The Days Scud By

The days scud by like leaves
Blowing by in the wind .
Our life is a enigma
We cannot comprehend

Peace of mind cannot be found
In knowledge for it is a wraith
It can only be found
Where there is a profound abiding faith

Faith that the sun will rise
Next 'morn flaming and robust
And the rain will continue
To fall on the just and the unjust

Faith that the one who made us
Has a plan that eventually
Will find a blissful fruition
In a place called eternity

Robert Richey

<u>The Fray</u>

There comes a time in Life
When there are no more mountains to climb
No more crevices to be crossed
For they are relegated to a previous time

There comes a time in life
When there are no more V.I.P.'s to greet
No more early morning commutes
On a busy road or a crowded street

There comes a time in life
No more worries about profit or loss
No more swallowing ones pride
By kowtowing to the boss

There comes a time in life
No worry about getting to work late
Or joining fellow Workers
On the usual coffee break

There comes a time in life
No more jumping up at the crack of dawn
No more sitting at one's desk
Struggling to stifle another yawn

And yet with all the frustrations
And worries of the work day
Sometimes, somewhere, some way
I miss being no longer in the fray

The Immaculate Birth

It Happened over two millenniums ago
In a land caressed by the sea
The miracle of that virginal birth
Transformed humanity

The wisemen and their camels
From the east had traveled afar
Guided by the constancy of
A bright and shining star

It had been forecast long ago
Perchance since time began
That the Messiah would be born
In the city of Bethlehem

The babe in swaddling clothes
Rested peacefully in the straw
While the Magi's gazed at him
In wonder and in awe

The gifts that they bestowed
Fruits of the journey they had made
Were of frankincense and myrrh
Gold and jewelry of jade

In the outer darkness the shepherds
Resting with their herds nearby
Gazed upward apprehensively to
The hosannas in the sky

Robert Richey

The son of man cannot be found
From delving into things apart
But can only be found
Within each troubled heart

The Olive Wreath

Lost in the mist of antiquity
Transcending time and temporal space
It's intrinsic strength perpetuity
Oblivious of clime or even race

Constant as the Pharaoh's Tombs
Brooding symbols of man's upward march
Footstep traces whose earthly wounds
Herald 'The Passing of the Torch'

Down thru the hallowed corridors of time
The Flower of mankind's young
Has bested, tested, striven and strived
To breast the tape, to vault the rung

With a primal need to lead the rest
Unwilling to bear the loser's cross
Averse to settling for second best
Or rely on the quirk of a coin toss

Urged ever onward toward a distant goal
Where no dream thing seems too far
Like standing up, and straight a tip-toe
Reaching, stretching to touch a star

No Golden Crown their just reward
No priceless bauble from the earth beneath
No treasure trove to grasp and guard
Their Holy Grail the Olive Wreath

45

A torch passed from hand to hand
All the day and through the night
O'er the mountains and across the land
In the light of day and out of sight

The steady pounding of the feet
Human frailty must not delay
Despite the panting breath, the heaving chest
The passing of the torch relay

The fabric of a valiant vanished race
Inextricably interwoven in the torches flames
Found expression in an awe inspiring tapestry
The acme, the apex, the pinnacle of

The Olympic Games

The Open Sea

Out where the Dome of the sky is Vast and Wide
Out where Vistas are as far as the eye can See
Out where the white caps dazzle the eye
Out where the billows roll on endlessly

Out where the dophins gambol and play
Out where the ships are tempest tossed
Out where the wild waters rage
Out where soars the albatross

Out where the codfish teem
In vast numbers from dawn to dawn
Out where the predatory shark prowls
Out where the salmon arrows back to spawn

Out where the tuna roams wild and free
Out where the saury and the sculpin abound
Out where the whale's watery breath erupts
Out where it pauses now and then to sound

Out of sight of the nearest land
Out where the sky is the deepest azure blue
Out to a place undefiled by the hand of man
Out where the sea is the richest of indigo hue

Out at sea on the darkest of nights
Out where the stars in the firmament seem on fire
Out where the flying fish glide from crest to crest
Out where is found the fulfillment of all desire

Robert Richey

Out where beauty reigns supreme
Out where power maintains ascendency
Out beyond the reach of any man made law
Out where I long once more to be!

Thats Life Far, Far Out on the Open Sea
A Place of Infinite Beauty

<u>The Way Life Is</u>

For every ounce of pleasure
There is an ounce of pain
For every sunshiny day
There is one drenched with rain

For every battle that we win
There is one we will surely lose
Trying always to be a winner
Is something we cannot choose

For every moment of happiness
There will be times when we are sad
It seems there is no formula
That will always make us glad

We can only take life the way it comes
Just living it day by day
For there seems there is no choice
Or that there is any other way

Perhaps the secret of living
Whether we are happy or sad
Is just to learn to smile
Through the good times and the bad

The Parade

They say the battle is the payoff
But we can only do our best
At playing the cards fate has dealt us
And hold them closely to our chest

But we cannot realize our potential
If we stand apart from the fray
And never get to hold the trophy on high
If we fail to carry the day

For Life is more than a destination
A multitude of stops it entails
The heavens may provide the winds
But we must adjust or trim our sails

However, If our goals are not lofty
Limited only by how hard we may try
We shall be in the Vanguard of Losers
And the Parade will have passed Us by

The Man from El Paso

There was a man from El Paso
And he wore his gunbelts way down low
He had a slow Texas drawl
But he was fastest on the draw!

One day Wild Bill was challenged
By a gunslinger named McGraw
When Bill reached up to scratch his head
McGraw beat him to the draw

They had a fancy funeral
With all the trimmings for Wild Bill
He now is a permanent resident
In a plot atop Boot Hill

We're gonna miss your kind of feller
We're gonna miss you Wild Bill
But if you hadn't stopped to scratch your head
Why, You'd be with us still, Bill

Wild Bill!

<u>The Seed</u>

It is nice to know in time of need
When one is filled with doubt and fear
To recall the tiny mustard seed
For it too does not 'know' why it is here

Although the tiniest of all seeds
Each one no more than a speck of dust
It yet strives its Creator to heed
To achieve whatever destiny it must

Hope also like a tiny seed
May germinate within the soul
And serve to satisfy a need
Allowing its flower to unfold

The flower from hope that doth arise
And flood the heart with joy and peace
Is faith that opens the believers eyes
And helps their grief and pain to cease

And so when one is filled with doubt and sorrow
And it seems there is no way to assuage the need
Then worry not today about the morrow
Think on Him who made the tiny mustard seed

<u>The Storm Raging About Us</u>

If your heart is heavy
And bowed down with grief
Then think on him who made you
If you would find relief

If the storm has raged about you
And cast your belongings to the winds
You will find comfort knowing that
If you believe, he has forgiven all your sins

If you have just lost your sweetheart
And are as full of doubt as you can be
Just remember he walked on the water
And with a word, Calmed the angry sea

"Let not your heart be troubled"
He said, and this he said too
"In my Father's house are many mansions
And there is one waiting there for you"

And if life has bruised and battered you
With all its ills and harms.
Remember our Father is waiting over there
For you with open arms

Robert Richey

The Sunset

Sunset far out on the open sea
Is wondrous to behold
With all the colors of the rainbow
Intermingled with the gold

A rhapsody of coloration
Esthetically sublime
An ethereal image
Created by a hand divine

As the sun sinks in the west
The colors shift from the view
Of orange, rose and red
Into the spectrum blue

Like banners gently waving
The consummate way
Before the sun has set
Of ending yet, another day

As the mauves and greys begin to fade
Like all the things we hold most dear
It is by faith alone we know
Come 'morn, the sun will reappear

<u>To the Millennium</u>

May the year that lies ahead of you
Be filled with joy and peace
May your troubles fade away
And may your happiness increase

When you wake each morn
And sense that dawn is near
Greet it like the farmer's friend
Bold chanticleer

And if a friend is lonely and sad
And bowed down with grief and care
Then put your arms about them
To reassure them that you are there

Greet others in a pleasant manner
And with a cheerful smile
And if they need a friend
Walk with them the extra mile

It may make for a banner year
If we follow the rule, tried and just
Of, Always do unto others
As you would have others do unto Us

<u>To Jeannie</u>

You are everything in life to me
You are my hope and my destiny
I'm enamored with all your lovely charms
I'm happiest with you nestled in my arms

Without you in my warm embrace
The world becomes a cold and lonely place
But all my troubles seem to disappear
When above all else I know that you are near

All lifes tribulations I can abide
As long as I know you are by my side
When you gaze deep into my eyes
I see only smooth sailing and sunny skies

I realized my greatest fantasy
The night you whispered that you loved me
And most of all what I said was true
That with all my heart I will always love you

I cannot bear to think of even one minute
In a world for me without you in it
For you are my hope and my destiny
You are everything in life, To Me

<u>What is Christmas?</u>

Christmas is more than a time of the year
More than a time of happiness and good cheer
It's more than experiencing a special kind of mood
More than just enjoying a lot of good food

It's Less about existing and more about living
Less about getting and more about giving
It's more about striving to make overdue amends
It's more about contacting many old friends

It's more than Christmas carols played fast or slow
Or even taking a sleigh ride over the deep snow
For Christmas is something brought down from above
It's about friends and family and most of all Love

Enigma

There is no Text Book in Life
That can make false that which is true
Yet can explain why grass is green
And even why the sky is blue

There is no Text Book in Life
To explain why lemmings drown in the sea
But can explain how to make lemon drops
And even how to brew sassafras tea

There is no Text Book in Life
To explain why it is water freezes
Yet can explain how to make antihistamins
To help all of us to stop sneezing

There is no Text Book in Life
To answer all the questions that plague us
Yet can tell us how to hedge our bets
When we play roulette in Las Vegas

But there is a Book of Life
Different by far than any before
That offers abolution from Sin
And to each of us Life Evermore

<u>Extinction</u>

Vast flocks of carrier pigeons
Used to darken the southern skies
The early settlers claimed that to them
Pigeons were more numerous than flies

And when they were asked why
They slaughtered all they were able
The reply to anyone who listened was
They needed them for the kitchen table

Carrier pigeons certainly were among
The dumbest of all the birds
Their irrational trust in the settlers
Went beyond common sense or words

While the pigeons were roosting
They would knock them in the head
And they kept right on aknocking
Until all of them were dead

One would surely think that
The settlers would've tried a different tack
That they would've surely understood
A vanished specie cannot be brought back

The Indians said in the early days
That the buffalo herds that passed
Were too numerous to count, it was
Like counting the blades of grass

But again the settlers guessed wrong
And not to anyones distinction
With 'Heroes?' like Bill Cody around
The herds approached extinction

The buffalo herds that roamed the plains
Whose droppings built the deep rich sod
Were all part of our national legacy
Most certainly a priceless gift from God

And that is not the end of the story
The problem just moved to a different place
After years of intensive over fishing
The cod fish disappeared without a trace

It still is not the end of the travail
The problem did not go away
The scene itself just merely shifted to
California off the coast of Monterey

The sardines that existed off the coast
Teemed in a truly vast number
But the fishing fleets applied themselves
In a classic case of mindless plunder

And so the sardine, the cod fish
Dinosaurs and flocks that used to be
Have all gone the way of the dodo bird
And vanished forever into eternity

The saddest part of all the above
Is that the world still has not learned
That there is no safe way to retreat
When all ones bridges have been burned

Politicians

There is one thing about Politicians
Whether they are from north, west, east or south
They all have one capability of
Talking out of both sides of their mouth

Of course they're not often prone
To spread gossip or even tattle
But on the other hand
There is no fence they cannot straddle

They are good at making speeches
And promise the voters the moon
Thats all very well and good
But times come to deliver it's another tune

Of course if they didn't play the game
And instead make the voters wait
Then next election time they would
Find that they had been given the gate

So is it really the politicians
That have their heads in the sand
Or is the basic problem
The voters who make demands

It has been said many a time
That elected officials do not the public serve
Probably in the final analysis
We get the kind of government we deserve

Progress

Our rivers and streams are polluted
The air is contaminated with smog
Our farm land is being eroded
It leaves one senses all agog

Offshore drilling continues
Oil spills our beaches befoul
Loggers continue destroying
The habitat of the spotted owl

Dead zones exist in the ocean
The sea with sharks blood runs red
With all these problems around us
Makes one reluctant to get out of bed

Danger lurks even on the highway
In the paper it's on every page
All drivers are increasingly in danger
Being victims of mounting Road Rage

It matters not which Party is in power
Or who actually is throwing the dice
If this is the price paid for Progress
Is it really worth the full Price?

Robert Richey

Reaping the Whirlwind

Childhood is certainly changing
As early as age eleven or twelve
They go out and shoot other students
Before turning the gun on their self

Lovers swear eternal devotion
To be there for better or worse
But then they break their promise
And go out and file for divorce

Politicians promise the voters
That there will be pie in the sky
But when it comes time to deliver
They just tell another white lie

Honesty is no longer in fashion
Courtesy and decency are old hat
But when everyone's making money
Why worry about something like that

Now success itself is exciting
It surely gives the Ego a boost
But there's one thing thats certain
Chickens always come home to roost

Of course there are nagging questions
But they can be ignored or placed on a shelf
However someday somewhere everyone
Will be forced to live with themselves

<u>Sayings...</u>

The cold war was a'raging
It's hand maiden was dread
Some even advocated
Better red than dead

By the bomb they were traumatized
Filled with fear and with fright
Ready to throw in the towel
Without even a token fight

But then just like in Jericho
The Wall came tumbling down
There was a wild celebration
The drinks were on the town

Then there was Napoleon Bonaparte
Who strutted like a prancing Stallion
He was heard to say one day that
"God's on the side of the Strongest Battalion"

But Nappy headed East as it seemed best
Perhaps some would even like to know how
Napoleons Grand Armie bled to death
In that cold unforgiving Slavic snow

Of course fighting in the Winter
Will always be bad news
If it has to be that way be sure
And take along your snowshoes

Then there was Julius Caesar
Who won many and many a 'bout'
He once said Vin-I, Vid-I, Vic-I
After kicking their stuffing out

When he came home after being away
Thinking of the many battles he had won
He said...Se Dice
Before crossing the Rubicon

However he too came a crupper
But it wasn't by his volition
He said "Et Tu Brute" as
They used him for a pin cushion

The thing to always remember
Is first always do your best
But when you're in bad company
Wear your bullet proof vest

Along came Winston Churchill
A man not won't to heed of his fears
He told the English public All I can
Offer you, Blood, Sweat and Tears

But then when it was all over
And he couldn't contribute anymore
Once the Boogie Man was dead
They showed him the door.

There was a man named Dempsey
A Manassa Mauler in a fight
He used to beat the pulp out of them
With his left hand or his right

But when he met Gene Tunney
He quickly ran out of luck
When the fight was over he said
"I guess I forgot to duck"

So If you are ever backed into a corner
And you're really getting beat
Always leave the back door open
So you can make a hasty retreat

The moral to this 'story' is
Though the Pens mightier than the Sword
Remember that when all is said and done
Actions speak louder than even the spoken Word

Robert Richey

The Highway To Success

They say the highway to success
Has too many bumps to mention
And that the road to hell itself
Is paved with good intentions

They say the way to get ahead
The surest way of them all
Is to just step up to the plate
And keep your eye upon the ball

They say to reach the top
The greatest way to be found
Is just to lean far, far over
And keep your ear to the ground

They say the shrewdest way of all
Is never fail your skills to hone
Forget about most everything else
And keep your nose to the grindstone

They say the answer to success
The best one you will ever find
Is just jump out of bed early
And enthusiastically rise and shine

They say the only way to gain
Where your efforts will not go kaput
Is just to daily swallow your pride
And kiss the boss's foot

However if you've tried them all
And you are still at a total loss
The ironclad rule is just go out
And marry the daughter of the Boss!

Eternal Love

Her hair was a lovely auburn brown
She had a twinkle in her eye
When I happened to look at her
I felt taller than the sky

She was warm and wonderful
And so much fun to be around
I doubt if any other place on earth
Ever had so much happiness abound

My ardor was a thousand fold
It was that way when I was young
And it is still the same way
Even though today I am old

I fell in love with her
At a very early age
In my Book of Life
Her name is on every page

She used to play the piano
On many a Sunday afternoon
And we as a family
Would sing familiar tunes

Ours was a star-crossed encounter
Of destiny or perchance Fate
For you see she was my mother
But she died when I was only eight

My father walked the streets all night
Oh! how he sobbed and how he cried
While my Uncle and I walked with him
All night long one on either side

He kept reproaching himself
Over and over always saying the same
While his brother tried to comfort him
Saying, "Bob you are not to blame."

And when the sun came up next morning
It was so bright and oh so red
And I felt far older than my years
For I had not been to bed

Then all the friends and family
Came and gathered around
And soon we stood silently
While they lowered her into the ground

I was just a little boy
I didn't fully understand
But I wish today that I had held
My brother and sister by the hand

But I know she is waiting patiently
Somewhere far, far away
And I find comfort knowing
Our paths will cross again some day

Robert Richey

I do know it will be a joyous reunion
Somewhere past the stars above
And I will take her tenderly in my arms
And tell her of my undying love

And perhaps in the hereafter
Beyond the stars and the moon
We may all be again together
And sing those same familiar tunes

A Man Named Henry

There was a man named Henry
And he had this incredible dream
It was his all consuming passion
To build the Untimate Driving Machine

Well Henry worked long and often
And he burnt the midnight oil
But there wasn't anything in the past
To help him in this, his time of toil

All travel made before he came along
Had been made on or behind a horse
Just bouncing along in a wagon or buggy
Or many times it was even worse

Of course everyone has preferences
About some they were willing to talk
But they all agreed conclusively that
If there were choices, they'd prefer not to walk

Well Henry found out early
That starting anything from scratch
Wouldn't be any bed of roses
And maybe he had even met his match

Nobody had said it would be easy
Or that it would be a lot of fun
Of course there were no guarantees
That the silly thing would even run

73

And to make things even worse
After all that sweat and toil
What in the world would it run on
When there wasn't even any oil

There is an old saying as true as it can be
That says adversity makes one stronger
That says the difficult we do right away
But the impossible takes a little longer

He had to design and build a motor
A radiator, body and a frame
Then there were the wheels and rims
On his finances it put a strain

Of course Henry wasn't the type
In frustration to let out any howl
And he certainly wasn't the type
To stoop to throwing in any towel

There is one fact as true as it can be
If Henry had just done a bunch of talking
Instead of religiously kept a working
Then all of us would still be walking

After months of toil and sweat
And maybe even some tears
Henry was ready to take it out
And put it through it's gears

So Henry climbed behind the wheel
An Assistant valiantly did his part
But in spite of some mighty cranking
The fool thing just would not start

Finally they got it a running
Henry kept an eye out for any Cop
But the problem he now found was
He couldn't get the dang thing to stop

Now to keep that car running
A repair shop it would not require
All the owner needed was
A roll of tape, pliers and bailing wire

With just those things handy
He wouldn't have any fears
Cause he could keep it running
For years and years and years

Fortunately he finally worked out
Any problems he could find
That is why today you and I
Can drive with peace of mind

At the job of building model T's
Henry had acquired a real knack
Customers could have any color car
They wanted, as long as it was black

Robert Richey

And by the way Henry
We hold this positive point of view
And we've decided you were quite a Man
And we are mighty proud of You

Growing Old

Growing old is not much fun
Just ask anyone who has been that route
They will tell you unequivocally
That's one thing where they have no doubt

But one finds when they are growing old
Regardless of how much they raise their voice
Getting down to the final analysis of it all
Do they ever really have any other choice?

For time moves on and on and on
There is just no way to stop the clock
We can fret and fume all we want
But the clock just keeps going tick, tock

But what other choice does one have
Resenting it matters not a whit
After all what anyone can really do
Except just try to grin and bear it?

Lost in Antiquity

Old as the redwood forest
It's roots deeper in the sands of time
Than those of the giant Sequoias
In the rocky soil of the Sierras

Indestructible as the Pyramids
Enigmatic as the face of the Sphinx
Tantalizing as the Egyptian hieroglyphs
Fascinating as the smile on the Mona Lisa

The Olympic Games of Antiquity
A game? Yes, but more than that
For the Olympics are more than a game
More than a test of athletic skills

Rooted in the elemental will to strive
In the primitive drive to dominate
In the eternal struggle of mankind
To cope with the one's inner self

The fascination of compelling
The body to do what the mind wills
To drive oneself to the limits of endurance
And then beyond those perceived limits

The never ending inner struggle within
The mind and heart of the Young, the strong
To be the best, to excel, to aspire
To stand upon the 'mountain top'

To climb a mountain 'because it is there'
To hangglide in treacherous winds
To venture into the unknown of space
To experience the feeling of exhilaration

Only the brave, the strong, the bold
Venture out of the zone of safety
Steeling themselves against
Their fears and superstitions

Archie

Archie Twiddle had an ego
Big enough for two
Archie thought there wasn't anything
That Archie could not Do

After a bit of contemplation
Archie conceived of a notion
He thought that Archie was the one
Who could invent Perpetual Motion

When his friends heard about it
They reacted with hoots and jeers
They said to Archie rudely
You couldn't do that in years

But Archie paid no heed to them
And worked with might and main
Archie was sure that all his work
Would not be all in vain

Archie spent many a night and day
And burned the midnight oil
But he only had zilch
To show for all his toil

Finally he had to admit
To everyone under the sun
That what he had attempted
Even by Archie could not be done

The Alamo

There is a place in west Texas
That they call the Alamo
It's in a part of Texas
Where not many things ever grow

The tree that grows the best there
It's name all who live there know
In English it is called cottonwood
In Spanish it is called Alamo

It happened in the year 1820
Southerners who were willing to go
Were invited to migrate to Texas
If they became citizens of Mexico

Many families from Alabama
From Mississippi and Tennessee
From Georgia and the Carolina's
Moved to make a new country

Unfortunately they were a stiff necked lot
Filled with pride and discontent
And they objected to trial without jury
Without any voice in the government

It wasn't very long before they found
With the Mexican Government they had words
And very soon it became apparent that
Both sides were more than willing to cross swords

General Santa Anna, the new dictator
Decided that he'd bring Texas to it's knees
And so he put his army on the march
To destroy this challenge to his authority

The only thing that blocked his path
The only obstacles where he aimed his blow
Was the small west Texas town of Goliad
And the mission called the Alamo

The Alamo was a structure made out of stone
It was manned by a hearty band
Bold adventureres who knew how to shoot
And were each loyal to each other to a man

Colonel Travis drew a line with his sword in the sand
Saying Anyone leaving cross to the other side
No man in the group moved forward
Not one man even considered it or complied

Those within the Alamo numbered only 182
Against Santa Anna with 3000 when he arrived
It seemed with so few defenders to resist
How the Texans could ever hope to survive

W. Barret Travis the Commander of the fort
When he received the order to surrender on the spot
Without hesitation, he ordered his cannoners
To defiantly respond, by firing a cannon shot

When the Texans refused to surrender

The black 'No Quarter Flag' was hoisted high
At Santa Anna's stern command
As the defenders of the fort prepared to die

The Texans already had the news
Of the enemies massacre at Goliad
So they were under no illusions
As to what fate they too would have

No quarter was asked or given
They were denied any desperately needed rest
The fighting and the dying continued
It obviously was a struggle to the death

The battle started with furious cannonades
The din and the destruction rained about
There was no rest or succor for those on either side
Tho' the defenders knew the issue was never in doubt

The struggle raged both day and night
The battlefield was covered with the dead
As the buzzards circled patiently high overhead
The wounded quietly and painfully bled

The siege started on February 23,1836
It continued unabated while both sides bled
On March 15 the Alamo itself was stormed
And taken, and all the defenders were dead

There is no cemetary at the Alamo
No place to hold a solemn ceremony

Robert Richey

No graves at which to place any flowers
As a tribute to their sacred memory

When the Alamo had been taken
And the last defender did expire
They were stripped of their clothing
And their bodies were consumed on the pyre

But if you happen to travel in Texas
It doesn't matter to which part you may go
Even today you will hear the battle cry
Remember Goliad! Remember the Alamo!

On the Prowl

Lurking in the depths of the forest
Moving furtively and silently like the owl
With a lean, gray and hungry look
A predatory wolf pack on the prowl

Nostrils quivering with anticipation
Testing each zepher coming their way
Searching for the stray vagrant scent
That would alert them to their prey

And with the deer, elk or moose
Peacefully and incautiously grazing still
The Pack coldbloodiedly and callously
Circled around and closed for the kill

With a rush they overwhelmed It
Slashing and tearing it all around
With their fangs embedded deeply
They pulled their victim to the ground

Ravenous in their pent up hunger
Growling and snarling at those nearby
They rend and tear at the carcass
Until their ravenous needs they satisfy

The predator is most powerful
And overpowering in every way
But by the quirks of survival
The predator may become the prey

Lobo, the dominate leader of the pack
Picked up a tantilizing scent one day
And proceeded to Leave the pack behind
For the scent led him far astray

He chanced upon a cache of meat
Dangling from the branch of a tree
It was easily within his reach
But it made him uneasy

His caution urged him to leave
That other game would be had
But game had been scarce lately
And his hunger drove him mad

Hesitantly he stepped forward
A searing pain, one he had never known
Suddenly had him in its grip
As the steel trap bit into the bone

Lobo struggled valiantly
In desperation he lunged about
But it soon became apparent
The paw would not come out

And so in pain and suffering
To escape from the traps maw
He agonizingly proceeded
To gnaw off his own paw

Painfully he then hobbled
On three legs once he was free
And then found shelter
Under a nearby low hanging tree

Meanwhile a member of the pack
Of Lobos absence became aware
And alerted the other members
That Lobo was no longer there

After a lengthy search they found him
But realized they could not stay
So after much whining and nuzzling
They proceeded on their way

Lobo's mate, Lupina, stayed with him
She whined and nuzzled him in vain
Trying in her own way
To help Lobo in his pain

The skies began to darken
A mighty wind blew through the trees
The temperature began dropping
And soon the rain began to freeze

When the sun came up next morning
Lobo had only one friend
For Lupino had stayed with him
Until the very end!

Robert Richey

<u>Troubles</u>

You cannot drown your troubles
They may be more durable than you think
If that is the route you finally choose
You'll find that troubles never sink

If you try to drown your troubles
Thinking you will be in clover
The chances are instead of that
You will wind up with a hangover

If troubles cannot be drowned
Then what is one to do?
Maybe 'tis better to work at them
And make them mighty few

Since troubles cannot be drowned
Instead of being faint hearted
Wouldn't it have been much better
If the troubles were never started?

Perhaps the way to avoid troubles
Instead of winding up in the red
Is to do things more deliberately
And just to always plan ahead

Lincoln Center

There is a place called Lincoln Center
That a lot of Seniors attend
They go there to play Bridge
In a place called Willow Glen

They meet there every Wednesday
A few minutes after noon
And they set up the tables and chairs
In a set pattern around the room

Each table has two decks of cards
A Score Sheet and a Pen
And the players use the bidding system
That they best comprehend

Each player has a partner
And uses the system they understand
And the bidding then tells the partner
The size and shape of their hand

They donate a quarter at each meeting
And it's all put in the pot
One must admit by todays standards
Thats not an awful lot

But when there are enough quarters
There's probably no one there whose rich
They take the money and go out
And buy a six foot Togo's sandwich

They cut it into slices
And add all the trimmings they need
And then each one takes their share
And have themselves quite a feed

After four games have been played
Of course to them it's old hat
Winners move to the next table
And losers stay where they are at

Now everyones there to have fun
It doesn't matter if they lose or win
But it sure is a fine way
To get better acquainted with them

Now every group needs a leader
And Ilse is the one they prefer
And she does such a fine job
That they are very happy with her

My wife Jeannie and I are long time members
And we try to regularly attend
But we don't go there just to play Bridge
We go there to visit with our Friends

<u>Why is it…?</u>

Why is there never time
To do something right
When there is always time
To always do it again?

Why is there never time
For things we call virtue
When there is always
Time for things we call sin?

Why is there never time
To extend a hand to a 'brother'
When there always seems to be
Enough time to attack one another?

Robert Richey

<u>A Small Frog</u>

I have never been
The Quarterback in the Huddle

But I have been
A Small Frog in many a Big Puddle

<u>To Jeannie</u>

Poets sing the praises
Of the earth and the sky above
Of the mountains and the prairie
And of hope and truth and love

I know not the thoughts of others
Or what may be their point of view
I only know the things which I find
In my own life always to be true

I'm happy when you are near me
And so sad when you are away
An hour with you seems like a second
A second without you seems longer every day

I eagerly look forward to seeing
A smile on your lovely face
The greatest comfort I can find
Is in your warm embrace

When you are away I'm lonely
Awaiting the sound of you at the door
And when I hear it open wide
How could I ever ask for more

When you're away out shopping
The house is a cold and lonely place
It's just not the same without you
Or without your lovely smiling face

But when you step inside it
The house becomes a home
The invisible tie that binds us
Makes me reluctant to ever roam

If I could have but one wish come true
It would be obviously plain to see
That we be sweethearts and lovers
Throughout all of eternity

And if only that prayer could be granted
I would not dare to ask for more
For I'd find all the joy and happiness
That fate could ever hold in store

<u>Kingfish</u>

Back in the bayou country
Where parochial feelings were strong
There was a man they called the 'Kingfish'
But his real name was Huey P. Long

Huey was the Governor
Of the state of Louisiana
And everybody in that state
Knew Huey was the top banana

They say Huey was no ladies man
He was never known to be flirty
And that Huey believed passionately
Politics was meant to be down and dirty

They say Huey never was a dancer
Or ever wore ballet shoes or leotards
But one thing he was never without
That was his army of bodyguards

They say when he mounted the stump
His speeches were full of frittle frattle
But every voter found out quickly that
There was no political fence he could not straddle

They say when constituents saw him
They would shout, "A rooty toot toot"
They all loved Ol 'Huey' cause
They say Huey always shared the loot

95

They say Huey was a bonafide product
Of a place called the deep south
And he found out early in his political infancy
To talk out of both sides of his mouth

They Say Huey's sensibilities were as thick
As a couple of buffalo hides
And right in the middle of any debate
He would try to back both sides

They Say Huey was no paragon of virtue
Or completely devoid of sin
And that to him the cardinal rule was
Do whatever it takes to win

They say no one had ever heard of his
Leaving some girl's heart aflutter
For in his Louisiana barroom politics
He got right down in the gutter

One day in the Court House in Baton Rouge
Of this there is no doubt
He got separated from his bodyguards
And a Doctor named Carl Weiss took him out

The Bodyguards then shot the assailant
They used on him a ton of lead
He was shot sixty one times
And another doctor pronounced him dead

They gave Huey a fancy funeral
With plumed horses and hearse so hard to beat
They paraded poor Huey up and down the town
While playing music all along Basin Street

They say Huey has gone to his reward
But Saint Peter may not know
And that if he isn't careful
Huey may wind up running the show

They say when you get to the Pearly Gates
Hang on to your wallet and keys
Cause Huey may well be there with a smile
Saying, "May I have your admission fee please?"

Now there are those who blame Politicians
While others blame the Public they serve
But there is one iron clad fact, and that is
The Voters get the Government that they Deserve!

<u>What I Long For</u>

I long for a different time
And for a different place
Where things were less hectic
And moved at a slower place

A place where mom and dad
Always stayed together
In the sunniest of times
And the stormiest of weather

A time when children knew
Through good times and bad
They could always depend on
Their mom and their dad

A time when children
Went to school for learning
And not for the reason
Of setting the place aburning

A time when I knew without a doubt
Right from wrong, virtue from sin
A time and a place vanished from sight
When I knew what I believed in

Those days are gone and will not return
Where they went I know not where
Confidence and hope have been replaced
With doubt, fear and even despair

<u>Hooked</u>

If anyone is contemplating
Hastening their own early demise
Then just buy a pack of coffin nails
And smoke them once or twice

They will find that they are misguided
Thinking it's the answer to their dream
But that's not the way it works
When tobacco gets into the bloodstream

Of course there are other benefits
That the user can soon tell
Because it isn't long before
Their tastebuds are gone as well

There is another matter to consider
And there isn't any answer
Because longtime use it has been found
Can ultimately lead to lung cancer

Non-smokers have all ganged up
And have conspired it's plain to see
Because all places of business
Are now required to be smoke free

But smokers feel they can afford them
They only cost nickels, quarter and dimes
And feel they can always quit puffing because
They've already quit a thousand times

<u>Every One Needs a Hero</u>

Every one needs a Hero
Perhaps now more than ever before

Every one needs a hero
One we can all unabashedly admire
Someone that we can always trust
And who will light our souls on fire

Everyone needs a hero
Of course Washington would lead the list

He and his brave men fought the British
And brought them to their knees
They were able to win the battle
Because they shot from behind the trees

Everyone needs a hero
But there are different points of view

The British General was quoted as saying
"It was a sticky wicket"
"It wasn't the way to fight, Ol' Bean"
"Why?, It wasn't even cricket"

Everyone needs a hero
Abe Lincoln of course comes to mind

Honest Abe said very firmly
His goal in life was the Union to save
Thats why he sent Grant and Sherman
Down south, to free all the slaves

Everyone needs a Hero
The Lone Eagle we must admire

When Charles Lindberg's plane took off
He told the onlookers not to be frantic
And then he flew right into history
When he headed out across the Atlantic

Everyone needs a Hero
Wrong Way Corrigan was his name

When Douglas lifted off the ground
Everyone believed what he said was so
But they were confused when he headed east
Instead of heading in the direction of Mexico

Everyone needs a Hero
Kilroy was his name

His name appeared in outrageous places
It appeared on boxes, crates, and ships
It has been stated unequivocally, that
At Normandy it was even on the cliffs

Everyone needs a Hero
The 'Sultan of Swat' we cannot ignore

With the bat on his shoulder he pointed
The crowd grew quiet and was very tense
When the pitcher delivered the ball dead center
Babe Ruth put it over the centerfield fence

Everyone needs a Hero
England was the land of his birth

What he was trying for, had never been done before
When he accomplished it, he had a radiant smile
Roger Bannister had just completed and run
In 3:59.4 seconds the first sub 4 minute mile

Everyone needs a Hero
Nearly everyone has been one at times

If a person has ever surmounted troubles
And faced them with enthusiam and zest
Then they certainly deserve the title of hero
If they have indubitably done their best

Everyone needs a Hero
Even those who are doing their job

Ty Cobb played baseball ferociously
There has never since been his likes
Whenever he set upon the bench
He set there a sharpening his spikes

Ty may have been called many a name
But he was never called a lemon
If anyone blocked the base path
Ty put his sharpened spikes in 'em

Everyone needs a Hero
Mothers of course would lead the list

They devote all their time and their energy
Certainly, as a group, they're sent down from above
And are always most considerate of others
For what they do is just done out of love

Everyone needs a Hero
Of course one may be greater than another

But the greatest hero of them all
The one American's will love the best
The one from the public sector
Is the guy that God will one day send
To abolish the tax collector

Happiness

Happiness is not a commodity
That can be bought and sold
It can not be quantified as
Being worth ounces of silver and gold

Happiness can not be reached
By extending our hand to clasp
If we approach it that way
It will always be beyond our grasp

Happiness is not something
That is always here to stay
It is the one thing to be enjoyed
It must be given away

Happiness cannot be found
By receiving diamonds and rings
But only realized by giving of ourselves
To others unselfishly on Angel Wings

Happiness can only be achieved
We have often been told
By bringing happiness to others
It will be returned a thousand fold

<u>Valhalla</u>

Will the roll be called one day in Valhalla?
Will the Vikings respond with a shout and a curse?
Will the sound of their raucous laughter
Echo throughout the Universe?

Will there be mountains and valleys in Valhalla?
Will there be trout streams and countless fiords?
Will Vikings still wear their horned helmets
And swagger about brandishing broadswords?

Will they be ministered to by the valkyries
Maidens with long blond tresses?
Will the Maidens still wear the traditional
And distinguishing Norwegian dresses?

Will there be oceans and seas in Valhalla?
Will their longboats be fitted with oars and with sails?
Will the Vikings still be permitted to raid and plunder
And do all the brutal things that entails?

Will they return home burdened with plunder?
Will they have captured maidens as their prize?
Will their homecoming be riotous as ever?
Will they all then happily fraternize?

Will the sun ever set in Valhalla?
Will the Northern Lights undulate on high?
Will the Vikings stand there in awe and wonder?
Wondering what it all doth signify?

Robert Richey

Will the Vikings get to see Thor and Loki
Norse Gods they have been taught to admire?
Will they get to greet Beowulf
The Norse King who put out the Dragons Fire?

However if Valhalla is found to be bucolic
And like the garden of Eden as well
Then to any red blooded Viking
It would be a special kind of hell

<u>Forsaken</u>

I thought God had forsaken me
I knew it must be so
But why did He let me share
Limpid mountain streams
And valleys blanketed with snow?

I thought God had forsaken me
I thought it must be true,
But why did He let me share
Birds and bees and butterflies
And skies of azure blue?

I thought God had forsaken me
That He was too busy up above,
But why did He
Send me a pretty Lass
Just for me to love?

I thought God had forsaken me
It was plain as plain can be,
But why did He
See that that Lovely Lass
Fell in love with me?

I thought God had forsaken me
For hours without end,
But why did He
When trouble seemed to strike
Always send by a Friend?

Robert Richey

I thought God had forsaken me
Even when I was tired,
But why didn't He
See that I managed
To get all the things I desired?

I thought that God had forsaken me
Right up to near the End
But then I finally realized that
God had not forsaken me
God had always been My Friend

The Hour Glass

The caravan wending onward
Across the burning shifting sands
The riders swaying rhythmically
Dreaming of far off exotic lands

The camels plodding forward
The sands blowing in their face
While the breeze swirling about them
Of their passage leaving not a trace

Among their precious cargo
Fruits of the journey they had made
Were frankincense and myrrh
Gold, silver and jewelry of jade

Caravans had crisscrossed
This forbidding 'sea' of desert sand
Far back into antiquity itself
Or so it seemed in the mind of man

The Pyramids along the Nile
The hieroglyphics upon their 'face'
The enigmatic smile on the sphinx
Bear testimony of a vanished race

Valiant People have come and gone
Driven onward with their insatiable lust
Each one has ruled and vanished
One by one disappearing into the dust

Then there appeared a fractious tribe
That lived in tents, beset by doubt and fears
And in this condition they wandered about
The desert, for all of the next forty years

They had a leader who was bearded and gaunt
One who had a haughty and patriarchal look
And with a resolve, fiercely insisted that
All people must live their lives by the book

This firebrand of a leader
Then climbed to the mountain peak
And there he received the tablets of stone
While there he heard God speak

He stood there in awe and wonder
Feeling like his mind had turned to mush
As he heard the voice of the Creator
Emerging from out of the burning bush

Then the voice that sounded like thunder
Told him he must unquestionably rely
Upon the rules engraved on the tablets
For they were the ones mankind must live by

Moses descended from the mountain top
Contemplating all the things he had been told
But he found to his own horror, his followers
Were now worshiping a calf made out of gold

In his fierce and righteous anger
With his temper completely out of control
Blindly he smashed the tablets of stone
And then destroyed the calf of gold

But God is not a god of infinite patience
That was one thing Moses came to understand
For while the rest of the people could enter
He was forbidden to enter the promised land

Over the span of thousands of years
Members of the tribe were made to understand
That the Law laid down through Moses
For eternity, it was to be the law of the land

There came a time in the tribe's history
When fate took on an unusual twist
They found themselves prone and helpless
Under the might of a Roman fist

One day a woman was taken in adultery
She and her partner were caught in the act
A crowd of angry people had gathered
To see that the law was observed, in fact

They had all gathered around her
Placing the blame on her and her alone
They were trying to work themselves up to
Being the first one to cast a stone

A tall stranger happened upon the scene

He was clothed in rustic raiment
There was a certain aura about his face
He inquired as to the charges content

Then he turned to the gathering and said
"Let he among you without sins to atone
One totally blameless in all that you do
Let such a one cast the first stone"

Then he kneeled down in their presence
And wrote with his finger in the sand
As they gazed at what he was writing
They individually came to understand

For the names and places that he sketched
Caused them to remember in shame
The transgressions that they had committed
For which they had not formerly been blamed

One by one they began to take their leave
Of righteous indignation they were all bereft
The gathering became fewer and fewer
Until finally all of them had left

The stranger stood up, looked about
And in the gentlest of voices said
"Where have thine accusers gone,
The ones who wanted you dead?"

She said" They've all gone Lord
But I am not sure why"

"Since they don't blame you"
He said, "Then neither do I"

And then he said like a benediction
"Woman live your life not like before
Rather it will be much better
If you go and sin no more"

The lesson we all can learn
It is not just for any of us alone
The important thing above all else
Is to not go around throwing stones

The Burleque...

He went to the burleque
The seats were nice and soft
The fellows were a shouting
"Rosie take it off!"

He went to the burleque
Breathing the smoke filled air
He went to the burleque
Just to sit back and stare

He went to the burleque
He went there many times
He went to the burleque
To watch the bumps and grinds

He went to the burleque
He went there more than twice
A sign over the door said
'No toucha da merchandise'

He went to the burleque
He wasn't really funning
He went to the burleque
To get his motor running

He went to the burleque
He went there and how!
He went to see Rosie 'cause
Rosie was the Cat's Meow

He went to the burleque
Rosie's bumping was a treat
She did a great big bump one night
A guy stage side, fell out of his seat

He went to the burleque
He had his tie and Tux on
He went to see Rosie
Cause she was the most buxom

He went to see the Burleque
There wasn't anything to bring
One night to his surprise, Rosie
Strutted about twirling her G-string

He went to the burleque
It didn't take much of a brain
He quit going 'cause the doctor said
He was suffering from severe eye strain

Robert Richey

Matey

Ahoy there Matey
We sail with the tide
To board yon vessel
Now lying broadside

We'll capture her crew
And divvy her plunder
We'll haul down her colors
Or perish by thunder

Be there Matey
or
I'll slit your gizzard

<u>This Game Called Life</u>

In this game called life
We are dealt a new hand every day
And like it or not
It's the hand we have to play

It seems the opponents get all the luck
That the gods of chance can bring
While my partner and I just shake our heads
As our hands point wise don't have a thing

And then when the hand is strong
There seems no chance to win
When the dummy hand is laid down
It is so weak it's almost a sin

But in the Game called Life
It we are ever going to get to the promised land
Will it ever be because of the cards we're dealt
Ot will it be the way we played the hand?

<u>A Fathers Grief</u>

He was my pride, and he was my joy
He was such a bright, handsome little boy
My heart was full right up to the brim
When with pride I happened to look at him

Although the world was full of toil and strife
I was so very grateful he came into my life
My hopes and dreams for him were plain to see
I wanted for him all the things life had denied me

And so as little boys do he grew in stature and grace
Always so happy and with a smile upon his face
Whenever he thought of something exciting and new
He would always say, "You know what?" to you

And you would say to him, "No, What?" in reply
Then he would share something exciting he had espied
Oh not hearing him say that again makes me so sad
Longing to hear him say, "I've missed you Dad"

Now it is all part of yesteryear
Those memories that I now hold so dear
A part of a past that will never return
It matters not how much I may yearn

Those were the truly happy times
But swept up in toil I failed to divine
But now that they are part of the past
To those dear memories I still hold fast

If only he could be small just once more
If I only could open up times door
Protecting him again from all lifes harms
And hold him again tenderly in my arms

Tho' we two shared winter, spring, fall and summer
Sadly we each marched to a different drummer
Unfortunately the birthright I so wanted him to claim
And his own ambitions were not the same

Somewhere, someway I know not how or when
I unintentionally and inadvertantly offended him
I wished I could correct the past and start anew
But once things are said they are impossible to undo

The years flew by but he was so far away
I kept hoping I would hear from him one day
And that we two could finally make our amends
And at the very least become good friends

Then one day I received a call by phone
The news I received left me cold and so alone
My son had been taken seriously ill betide
In fact so ill that he had almost died

I rushed down by plane as quickly as I could
And soon by his bedside apprehensively stood
I felt like on the cross I had been nailed
When I was told his kidneys had failed

When I held his hands too choked up to speak
I felt gaunt and old and oh so very weak

As I noticed that he looked that way too
He said, "I guess I have been mean to you"

And so I returned from whence I came
With a heavy heart feeling Iike I was to blame
Wondering in the past what I could have done
So I would not feel like I had failed my son

A short time later the phone rang again
A tearful voice spoke choked up with pain
The words I heard filled me with dread
The voice said simply "Our son is dead"

Perhaps we will meet again someday
It may be beyond Venus or even Mars
But then again it may very well be
Beyond the fartherest stars

You were my pride, You were my joy
You were such a bright, handsome little boy
Although the world was full of toil and strife
I was so grateful when you came into my life

My soul is bowed down in grief
I know no joy or even peace
Fate has smote me with more than steel
And left a wound that will not heal

I always tried to do what's right
I stayed the course, fought the good fight
God in thy infinite love and mercy
Why doth thou thus punish me?

<u>Deregulation California Style</u>

I live in Sunny California
The most populated State in the Nation
Where the citizens out here are upset
About all of this Energy Deregulation

I live in Sunny California
The Utility Companies think we are full of beans
Cause according to them
We insist on living beyond our means

I live in Sunny California
The Utility Companies think we are a louse
Cause according to them
We go around turning on every light in the house

I live in Sunny California
They want us to understand
That to provide us with electricity
They must go about hat in their hand

I live in Sunny California
They say our demands are unjust
And if things continue the same way
They eventually will have to go bust

I live in Sunny California
If they can't do their job with a flair
Then I guess we will just
Have to take our business elsewhere

<u>Longevity</u>

I'm setting here in this wheelchair
A setting here by the door
I sat here all day yesterday
I'll be setting here a lot of days more

Friends don't come to see me much
Of course not many are still alive
But that is what eventually happens
When you start pushing ninety five

Theres not much to keep me busy
Can't see to read the paper anymore
My hearings not getting any better
I'm getting pains and aches by the score

I get kinda tired of laying idly about
And tireder still paying all these bills
It seems every time I turn around
It's time to take some more pills

I can dimly remember having lunch
But can't remember what I had
It must have been pretty good
I'd probably remember it, if it was bad

The doctor says I've got bed sores
They are as black as they can be
It they get much, much worse

I may lose both legs below the knee

I've got lots and lots of relatives
And a bunch of nephews and nieces
But I'd rather God just took all of me
Instead of taking me in pieces

Robert Richey

Our Best Wishes

There is one irrefutable fact
At times we must all confess
The heart is a lonely hunter
Searching for happiness

But even in the Garden of Eden
Where from work there was a reprieve
Adam didn't find happiness
Until God created Eve

When the Ark itself was ready for
The elephant and even the kangaroo
All of the creatures that went aboard
Went aboard two by two

From this day forward
Whether the skies are gray or blue
Where ever your paths may lead
Our best wishes will follow you

May your lives together
Be free of care and stress
And we wish you and your beloved
Every happiness

And so may we take this moment
Your friends here at Willow Glen
To wish you joy together
And devotion that will never end

Bon Voyage as you venture
Out on the sea of life Together

Robert Richey

<u>The Thief upon the Cross</u>

Our life is like a vapor
Elusive as the clarion call of chanticleer
We emerge from the outer darkness
And one day quietly disappear

It matters not how convoluted be the concept
Or how intrically crafted be the plan
The legacies that we leave behind
Are like footprints in the sand

It matters not how mightily we strive
Or whether our cause itself be just
One day even the Pyramids
Will moulder into the dust

The only hope mankind has
Winnowing thru the chaff and dross
Is just to simply acknowledge His divinity
As did one of the thieves upon the cross

<u>Blue Helmet</u>

They say a war is araging in Bosnia
Others twixt here and far as old Bombay
Our soldiers are caught right in the middle
And can't shoot back either way.

I don't want to go to Bosnia
Or even to Tombouctou
I didn't swear that I would wear
A Helmet that was blue.

There's no cotton candy over there
No gum that I can chew
It's cold and wet and miserable
And the women are mighty few.

I don't want to go to Bosnia
Or even to Tombouctou
I didn't swear that I would wear
A Helmet that was blue.

If I don't try and follow orders
The Army has me understand
They will Court Martial me
And throw me in the can.

But I don't want to go to Bosnia
Or even to Tombouctou
I didn't swear that I would wear
A Helmet that was blue.

Robert Richey

Make no mistake, I love my counntry
And I'll protect her if I can
But I ain't gonna try and police the World
Why, they've got another think man,

Cause I don't want to go to Bosnia
And here I stand tall and true
For I didn't swear that I would wear
A Helmet that was blue.

<u>Heres to Friendship</u>

For each of us life is like
A stroll through time and space
Although there are times when
We must move at a slower pace

But along the way we marvel
At the Birds and the flowers and the bees
And glory in the blue sky above and
The welcome shade under the trees

Or stand there at the first light of day
In awe and wonder at what we see
A glorious panorama of color
Of a sunrise's pristine majesty

And we may walk along the way
In all kinds of weather
And then one day a merciful God
Brings our pathways together

And for a little while we share
A pathway we hope will never end
Because on this special pathway
We walk side by side with a Friend

And we just enjoy being together
And share out hopes and share our dreams
And talk about the exciting things of today
And what we hope tomorrow brings

But as the sunset always follows the dawn
And tho' each and every pathway ends
That doesn't mean that we can't remain
True, loyal and devoted friends

A Brief Biography of the Author

A problem with any literary effort of this sort is the question of, "Where does one begin?"

On my fathers side I am a fourth generation American. The limited information available indicates my greatgrandfather, as a young man, immigrated from Ireland during the potato famine. He and two brothers then settled in the southern state of Georgia. Apparently he then immigrated to a rural farming community located in northwestern Alabama.

When my father was a young adult the parents, his two older brothers and a younger sister progressively immigrated to Mississippi, then into Louisiana and finally settled in a small farming community east of Bryan, Texas. At that time it was considered the frontier.

A world away a young man grew up in Olso, Norway. As an adult he captained a ship that plied between Norwegian ports and various ports of call along the eastern seaboard and along the Gulf Coast.

He retired from the sea and settled in Algiers, a small seaport town across the river from the city of New Orleans. There he married my grandmother and my mother Magdalena, an only child, was born. My grandfather captained a number of river vessels on the Mississippi before finally retiring from the water.

The family then moved to the same farming community where my fathers family had located. My grandfather ran his own dairy.

My mother and my father met and were married in a small non-denominational church at a small crossroads called Steep Hollow

I was my fathers first child and was born near the waning days of the so called "Great War to end all Wars." My grandfather then died during the great flu epidemic that decimated nations worldwide.

When I was on 2 or 3 the family moved to a town on the Gulf called Port Arthur. In a year or so the family moved a few miles north to the city of Beaumont. This city fronts on a river with a 40 foot channel to the sea.

My sister was born two years after I was and my brother was born two years later.

When I was only eight years old our mother suddenly and unexpectedly died in childbirth. The two twin babies died with her. The family never recovered from that tragedy.

When I was only eleven years of age in 1929 the Stock Market crashed worldwide. The Banking System also collapsed due to the unwise excesses in the Stock Markets. The entire industrialized countries were then plunged into a decade long Economic Dark Age.

In this country millions of men lost there jobs and their means of earning a living. Countless numbers of men rode atop boxcars vainly seeking work. They grubbed out an existence living in Hobo Jungles and selling apples on street corners.

I managed to pay my way through two years of junior college by delivering newspapers on a paper route. I delivered 124 papers morning and evening and had to collect for the papers. I only earned about a dollar a day and many times walked 8 miles doing so.

After finishing the two years and with no employment opportunies in sight I applied for and passed all the tests and enlisted for four years in the Regular Navy.

During the next four years I served in a Communications Division on Battleships. On the Battleship USS West Virginia I was assigned to an Admirals Staff.

In the fall of 1940, at the expiration of my four year enlistment, I left the navy and departed the Battle Force in Pearl Harbor.

On december 7, 1941 the pilots of Japans six big carriers attacked and virtually destroyed the battleships which were the backbone of the Pacific Fleet in Pearl Harbor.

In a short time I reenlisted in the Navy and was ordered to report aboard a new destroyer (The USS Woodworth DD460) being made ready for sea in the bay at San Francisco.

Several months later in the far Pacific this ship was assigned to Destroyer Squadron 12 which became part of Admiral Bill Halseys Third Fleet.

The Squadron was heavily involved in the early fighting in the Solomons Campaign. Of the fifteen ships that served in the Squadron in 1942-43 eight were sunk (The O'brien, Duncan, Meredith, Monssen, Barton, Laffey, Aaron Ward and Gwin. Many lives were lost). Many of the surviving seven destroyers suffered damage, some extensive, and loss of lives (Fahrenholt, the Squadron leader, Buchanan, Grayson, Lansdown, Lardner, McCalla and Woodworth, the one this author was on).

After the war this nation experienced a decade long period of turmoil as it struggled to return to a peace time economy. A vast number of young men returned from all the far flung battlefields unprepared for jobs due to the depression. Women and older men had manned the factories and defense plants and had acquired all the job skills so desperately needed by the returning Veterans. It was a truly stressful time in the history of this great nation.

This writer became a teamster in one of Jimmy Hoffa's biggest Unions on the west coast for fifteen years. It was a difficult and physically demanding profession at that time with few if any labor savings devices available. It was like they built the pyramids a grain of sand at a time.

The last seven years of the above mentioned fifteen this writer attended and graduated, with honors, from one of the Biggest California State Universitys in Engineering mid term 1963-64

My first job assignment in Engineering was on the Apollo Project as a Structural and Thermal Stress Analyst on the Apollo Command Module Heat Shield. I worked for three years for North American Aviation located in Downey, California and the Space and Information Systems Divisions. After a brief stint on another Space Program after the Apollo phased out the Space Program collapsed.

The Space community then was plunged into its on Dark Age where hundreds of thousand of former Aerospace Engineers and Technicians were cast out into the Jobless market. They were to specialized or too experienced in a job market that no longer needed their kind of expertise.

During my remaining work years I was a Traffic Engineer for eleven years where that part of the society struggled somewhat vainly to move people and goods efficiently and safely on the Nations highways with marginal success due to the ever increasing an inexorable demand. During this time I passed the test for Registration as a Professional Engineer In Traffic Engineering in the State of California.

My wife Jeannie and I have enjoyed retirement and being together with each other. Grateful for good health where we have been blessed with being able to join in the things we mutually share and have an interest in.

So what did I learn along this journey we call life? Well for one thing I learned how deeply the average American has always loved their country, with a passion. Also I have learned that it is a rare privilege to having been born an American. I have learned how well and wisely the founding fathers crafted our Constitution and the Laws that help maintain order in an ever changing world.

And a long time ago when the ship I was on made landfall just off the California coast at San Francisco in about the first week in March of 1944 I was excited as a small boy at a birthday party.

When I ventured topside just about daybreak to catch that first glimpse of San Francisco to my chagrin the fog was so thick I could hardly see ten feet ahead. As I stood there with that damp fog swirling about me and the ship proceeding slowly and cautiously under Radar control I could hear the fog horns on the bouys in the near distance. With my hands plunged deeply into my peacoat pockets I stood there on the bow of the ship peering through the fog.

Suddenly I heard a shout behind me and to my left, "There she is!!" I could see one of the crew on the port wing of the bridge pointing upward. As I turned and looked in that direction I saw probably the most beautiful sight I will ever see; there emerging through the fog was the Golden Gate bridge. It brought tears to my eyes and all I could think was, "Thank God I have been spared and I am home at last."

Printed in the United States
986000006B